DISCARD

jBIO
CARVER

Adler, David A.

A picture book of
George Washington
Carver.

BIOGRAPHY
CHILDREN'S ROOM

$15.95

DATE			

BAKER & TAYLOR

A Picture Book of
George Washington Carver

David A. Adler
illustrated by Dan Brown

Holiday House/New York

George Washington Carver was born a slave. He was never sure of his birth date, just that it was in 1864 or early 1865, near the end of the Civil War. He was born on the Missouri farm of Moses and Susan Carver, where his mother, Mary, was a slave.

George hardly knew his mother. When he was an infant, raiders kidnapped him and his mother and took them to Arkansas. A neighbor found George and brought him home, but he didn't find Mary. Young George Washington Carver never saw her again.

George's father was a slave, too, but George never met him. His father worked on a neighbor's farm and was killed in an accident around the time George was born.

George and his brother, James, were raised by Moses and Susan Carver. The Carvers were good to the boys. George called Mr. Carver "Uncle Mose."

George was not a strong boy. He wrote later that his body was in "constant warfare between life and death." The Carvers did not make him work hard on the farm. He fed the animals and helped Susan Carver around the house. He had plenty of time to swim and explore the nearby woods.

George had his own little garden. He wrote later, "I wanted to know every strange stone, flower, insect, bird, or beast," and "Many are the tears I have shed because I would break the roots or flower" off some of those "pets." But he hid his garden in the brush because, "It was considered foolishness in that neighborhood to waste time on flowers."

The Carvers wanted him "educated the same as white children. . . . They taught me to read, spell, and write just a little."

George needed to know more. His only book was a Webster's Elementary Spelling Book. He read it so often, he "knew it by heart." But that book had few answers for him.

When George was twelve, he went to a school for African-American children in nearby Neosho. There he lived with Mariah and Andrew Watkins, a black couple. He paid for his room and food by helping around the house.

His "aunt" Mariah was a nurse. George learned from her which plants and herbs cure illnesses. She also taught him the value of time. Even during school recess, he had to run home to help Mariah with the laundry. There was no time for play.

The teacher in the Neosho school did not know much more than George. After less than a year there, George felt he needed to move on. He found a family on its way to Fort Scott, Kansas, almost one hundred miles away, and he hitched a ride.

In Fort Scott, George went to school, worked in a nearby grocery, and did laundry for people staying at the Wilder House, a hotel. He lived with a blacksmith and his family and helped out there, too.

In March 1879 in Fort Scott, a mob of masked white men pulled a black prisoner out of jail, tied him with a rope, and dragged him for five blocks. The prisoner was hanged and later burned. George Washington Carver witnessed that lynching and quickly left Fort Scott. The ugly memory of that night haunted George the rest of his life.

He went to Olathe, Kansas. From there he went to Paola, Kansas, and then to Minneapolis, Kansas, where he graduated from high school.

Carver still had what he called "the thirst for knowledge." In 1885 he applied by mail and was accepted to Highland University. But when he arrived to begin his studies, he was told that he could not attend the school because he was black.

George Washington Carver changed his plans. He became a farmer and bought land farther west. He built a one-room sod house with walls made of thick chunks of grassy dirt and a roof made of tar paper and dirt. He planted vegetables, studied art, and made friends.

But he became restless. He still had his thirst to learn. Carver traveled east to Iowa, and in September 1890 he enrolled in Simpson College. He was the school's first African-American student. He studied art there, but soon realized he could do more for his people working with plants. He transferred to Iowa State College, where he studied agriculture.

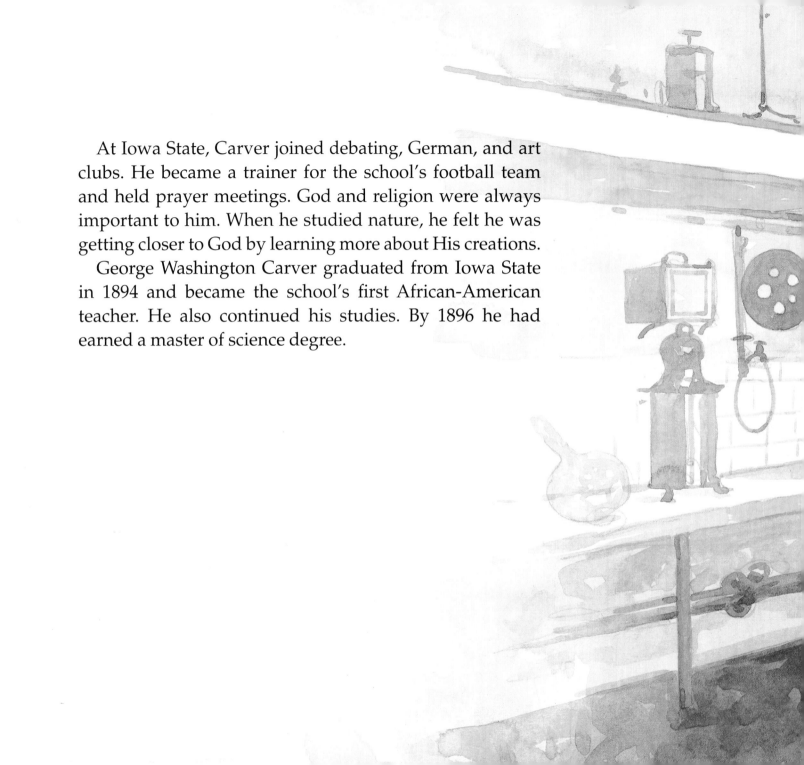

At Iowa State, Carver joined debating, German, and art clubs. He became a trainer for the school's football team and held prayer meetings. God and religion were always important to him. When he studied nature, he felt he was getting closer to God by learning more about His creations.

George Washington Carver graduated from Iowa State in 1894 and became the school's first African-American teacher. He also continued his studies. By 1896 he had earned a master of science degree.

In 1896 Booker T. Washington, one of the most respected African Americans of the time, asked Carver to join him at the Tuskegee Institute in Alabama. The school was established in 1881 to train African Americans for work, and George Washington Carver became the head of its department of agriculture. He lived and worked there the rest of his life.

Carver was devoted to improving the lives of Southerners, especially African Americans. Most of them were cotton farmers. Constant cotton planting ruined the soil, and in some years entire crops were destroyed by boll weevils, small beetles that left their eggs in cotton-flower buds. Carver was determined to find other crops that would grow well in the South and could support Southern farmers.

Carver found that peanuts and sweet potatoes improved the land and were not threatened by boll weevils. He called them "two of the greatest products God has given us." He knew Americans would not eat as many peanuts and sweet potatoes as Southern farmers could grow, so he looked for new uses for them.

In his laboratory, Carver separated the fats, gums, sugars, starches, and other chemical parts of the peanut.

He worked with these components and found some three hundred different peanut by-products, including peanut milk, flour, cheese, candy, ice cream, butter, shampoo, face cream, glue, wood stain, and ink. He even discovered that rubbing a certain kind of peanut oil onto the skin was helpful in treating polio, a crippling disease that often afflicted children.

He found he could make more than one hundred useful products from sweet potatoes, including flour, syrup, starch, a coffeelike drink, molasses, glue, vinegar, alcohol, and synthetic rubber.

George Washington Carver loved his work. He said, "Know science and science shall set you free, because science is truth."

Carver believed his discoveries came as a direct message from God and refused to accept any money for them. Sometimes he did not even cash his paychecks from Tuskegee. The great inventor Thomas Alva Edison offered Carver a huge salary to work for him, but Carver refused. He wanted to work only for the good of "his people," African Americans.

George Washington Carver believed in the goodness of all people, that "we are brothers, all of us." He felt that successful blacks, such as himself, should be models for others, who together would "transform the race in the eyes of the world."

Carver liked to say, "Save everything. From what you have, make what you want." In 1941 he displayed his handicrafts made of seeds, peanuts, and chicken feathers. Also in the Tuskegee exhibit were seventy-one of his paintings, many done with paints he made from vegetables, magnolias, and Alabama clay. *Time* magazine, in its review of the exhibit, called Carver the "Black Leonardo," a reference to Leonardo da Vinci, a genius in many fields.

George Washington Carver won many awards for his work. In 1923 the National Association for the Advancement of Colored People gave him the Spingarn Medal. In 1939 he was given the Theodore Roosevelt Medal for Distinguished Research in Agricultural Chemistry.

George Washington Carver died on January 5, 1943, at Tuskegee Institute. People from all over the world mourned his death.

IMPORTANT DATES

1864 or 1865	Born on a farm near Diamond Grove, Missouri
1886	Settled in Ness County, Kansas, and built a sod house
1891–1896	Studied at Iowa State College
1896–1943	Worked at Tuskegee Institute
1921	Appeared before a committee of the United States Congress and demonstrated the many uses of peanuts
1923	Awarded the Spingarn Medal
1939	Awarded the Roosevelt Medal
1943	Died on January 5 at Tuskegee Institute, Alabama

SELECTED BIBLIOGRAPHY

Berbman, Peter M. *The Chronological History of the Negro in America.* New York: Harper & Row, 1969.

Holt, Rackham. *George Washington Carver: An American Biography.* New York: Doubleday, 1960.

Kremer, Gary R. *George Washington Carver: In His Own Words.* Columbia and London: University of Missouri Press, 1987.

McMurry, Linda O. *George Washington Carver: Scientist and Symbol.* New York: Oxford University Press, 1982.

Peanut, Gene. *George Washington Carver: Botanist.* New York: Chelsea House, 1989.

AUTHOR'S NOTE

George Washington Carver's work first became widely recognized in 1921, when Carver appeared before a committee of Congress. Congress was considering a tariff on peanuts from other countries. The tax on imported peanuts would greatly benefit American peanut farmers. Carver demonstrated the value of peanuts by showing their many uses. Following his talk, the tariff was passed and Carver was famous.

Booker T. Washington said in an 1895 speech in Atlanta that every black should "cast down your bucket where you are." He believed blacks must work within the system. In many ways Carver's attitude toward race problems was close to Washington's. Carver wrote in 1937, "I am trying to get our people to see that their color does not hold them back as much as they think." Their attitudes were considered too accepting by more militant black leaders such as W. E. B. Du Bois, who felt blacks must demand equal rights.

To Kathy Tobiason, Jessica Swist,
and all my friends at A. S. I. J.
(The American School in Japan)
D. A. A.

To my son, Trevor,
with love and affection
D. B.

Library of Congress Cataloging-in-Publication Data
Adler, David A.
A picture book of George Washington Carver / David A. Adler;
illustrated by Dan Brown. — 1st ed.
p.   cm.
Includes bibliographical references (p.   ).
Summary: A brief biography of the African-American scientist who
overcame tremendous hardship to make unusual and important
discoveries in the field of agriculture.
ISBN 0-8234-1429-9
1. Carver, George Washington, 1864?–1943—Juvenile literature.
2. Agriculturists—United States—Biography—Juvenile literature.
3. Afro-American agriculturists—Biography—Juvenile literature.
[1. Carver, George Washington, 1864?–1943. 2. Agriculturists.
3. Afro-Americans—Biography.] I. Brown, Dan, 1949–   ill.
II. Title.
S417.C3A64   1999
630'.92—dc21
[B]   98-20261
                                                          CIP
                                                          AC